CAREGIVING AT A GLANCE

**A Fingertip Guide to Caring for a Loved One
with Memory Impairment**

Insight Memory Care Center
InsightMCC.org

This guidebook contains many ideas that have come from family caregivers during the last thirty years. Many of these people learned the hard way through trial and error while caregiving for a loved one. We are grateful to all of them for sharing their insights and suggestions.

Printing of this Fifth Edition was sponsored by the Max and Victoria Dreyfus Foundation.

Caregiving at a Glance: A Fingertip Guide to Caring for a Loved One with Memory Impairment.
5th Edition

Insight Memory Care Center
3953 Pender Drive, Suite 100, Fairfax, VA 22030
703-204-4664 | InsightMCC.org

Dedication

This book is dedicated to Lin Simon, founder of Insight Memory Care Center, and her incredible vision and passion to help. She inspired many along the way to make each moment meaningful for people living with memory impairments.

Thanks

Thanks first and foremost to the thousands of family caregivers who have shared their successful approaches with the staff of Insight Memory Care Center. You all are the real authors of this guide.

Many thanks to Lin Simon, Ph.D. for initially developing this guide. Thanks to Dan Sands, Shelley Gardner, Jim McCullough and Paul McCarty who reviewed and edited the original text. Thanks to Moira Shannon and Mac Showers who reviewed the 1st and 2nd editions.

Thanks to Blair Blunda, Shaquita Coleman, Anna Ellis, Mac Showers, Teresa Rollo, and Marilu Rivera for helping to update the 3rd edition.

Thanks to Nancy Vasser, Diana Bozza, Jane Hatfield, Kathleen, Pam, John, Marie, Estelle, and Lydia for helping to update the 4th edition.

And many thanks to Brigid Reynolds, RN, MSN, NP; Arvette Reid; Cynthia Sullivan, Ph.D.; Cathy Tompkins; Ken Wood; Christi Clark; and Carrie Idol-Richards for helping to update the 5th edition.

CONTENTS

FOREWORD

Have you ever looked through a kaleidoscope? If you have, you know that every time you turn the end of it you can see a new design, slightly different from the previous one. Yet, if you opened it up you would find a few chips of colored glass are the only ingredients responsible for all the different patterns that you see.

The effects of Alzheimer's disease on a person work much the same way as the kaleidoscope. The same plaques and tangles appear in brain tissue for those affected but the differences among individuals with these brain changes can vary tremendously. The variety of symptoms and behaviors that can occur add to the progressive nature of the illness and make it very difficult to write a concise guide on caregiving. In addition, what works today may not work tomorrow.

Compiled from all the helpful tips from families at Insight Memory Care Center, this guide is offered in a format that, hopefully, will make it easier for you as a caregiver to use on a daily basis.

INTRODUCTION

Now in its third decade of publication, Caregiving at a Glance remains a helpful tool for families and caregivers supporting individuals dealing with the struggles of Alzheimer's disease or other forms of dementia. Our hope remains that, one day, we find a cure and this guide becomes obsolete. Until that occurs, Caregiving at a Glance will continue to be a practical resource and guide for those caring for a loved one facing this life-changing challenge.

Inside this guide, we have compiled helpful hints and "aha's" we have heard from families at Insight Memory Care Center. While each individual's dementia journey is unique, we have found that using these techniques can empower you as a caregiver. Utilizing this guide will help you gain confidence and ease the burden as you walk alongside your loved one on their dementia journey.

Caregiving is both an art and a skill. Caregivers today are more knowledgeable about dementia and are using their creativity to solve complex dilemmas that previously seemed unsurmountable. In the quest to find a cure, research has provided us with more information about the physiology of dementia. This has led to new ways of identifying the disease even before noticeable symptoms have developed and offers hope that one day Alzheimer's disease and other dementias will be preventable. Though we have not yet found a cure, medications to help alleviate the symptoms of dementia are available. Finally, society has grown in its knowledge and experience, and a wider variety of resources, programs, and services is now available for individuals in all stages of dementia.

While progress has been made, there are still many challenges that exist in caregiving. We have not been able to eradicate the guilt and second-guessing that plague us as caregivers, but our hope is that this guide will help you feel more confident and capable as you provide care for your loved one. This guide is not intended to replace the wealth of information that is available online and through support groups, family physicians, and organizations such as Insight Memory Care Center. Its intent is to provide quick and easy explanations for why behaviors may appear and suggestions regarding what could make day-to-day caregiving easier.

Creativity, common sense, humor, and compassion are great strengths that you possess. You should use them on your caregiving journey. Many strategies that have worked wonderfully have been discovered serendipitously when all else failed. If you find yourself identifying with a particular situation in this guide, take it as an expression of comfort. Someone else has been there before you and many others will follow. You are not alone.

A Note of Encouragement from Mac Showers, Family Caregiver

If you are a caregiver confronting Alzheimer's disease for the first time, or if your loved one is still in the early stages of the disease, some portions of this guide may seem overwhelming. Please be assured that this document is prepared for the benefit of caregivers facing all levels or stages of the disease. Developments occur at variable rates - some slowly, some more rapidly. The same events don't always occur in the same order as each person is unique. This guide is intended to cover a variety of events to help you through some of the daily, weekly, and monthly changes you may see. You will be learning step-by-step, and will soon realize that your ability to keep pace with the disease is within your grasp.

OVERVIEW

Diagnosis Dementia…Now What?

Caregiving

Finding Additional Care

From a Family Caregiver

" I have a much better, and much more clear picture of where we're going, and what we need to do and consider, and the options we have along the way. "

DIAGNOSIS DEMENTIA... NOW WHAT?

A diagnosis of dementia can be overwhelming, stressful, or even a relief! But it always brings with it a wealth of questions, most of which are some variation of "now what?"

The following list includes practical suggestions that have helped many of our caregivers at the beginning of their journey. Just like Rome wasn't built in a day, this list cannot be completed in an afternoon. Many of these topics are also addressed in more detail throughout the guide. However, these suggestions can provide a good starting point for planning your next steps.

Plan for the future

- Educate yourself and your family about the disease.

- Find support for the person living with dementia and yourself.

- Look at what healthcare, legal and financial decisions you have to consider for the future. Each situation is unique, and you may need to involve a professional to ensure your needs are met.

- Involve the person living with dementia in all aspects of planning while they still have capacity.

- Familiarize yourself with resources before they are needed.

- What are your abilities and limitations as a caregiver?

Start the conversation

- Understand the disease. Learn more about your loved one's particular diagnosis and how it might impact your situation.

- Learn the importance of effective communication.

- Ask questions about your loved one's desires, and respect their wishes.

- Review your finances. Ensure that your plans will be feasible!

- Get your legal documents in order.

Develop a Care Team

- Family and friends can provide respite, support, and a listening ear.

- Make sure your healthcare providers are knowledgeable about the disease and/or find specialists to provide support.

- Find support from the organizations, community groups, or faith organizations you are already a part of, and research if other groups might be a good fit for you now or in the future.

- Professionals in their fields can provide a wealth of knowledge, especially for more complicated healthcare, legal, and financial decisions.

Make a plan

- Identify your sources of support, everyone from immediate family to trusted professionals.

- Discuss care values with your loved one as long as they are able, and the role they will play in future care.

- Share your preferences for care too!
- Communicate your plan to family members, so they can help support you along the way.

Find support

- Locate community resources; you may end up needing different resources throughout the journey.
- Consult a professional to make sure things are done right.
- Hire help before things get too challenging!
- Find housing with supportive services for if or when the time comes.

Care for yourself

- Balancing work and caregiving is tough. Make sure you don't pull yourself in too may directions.
- Understand the financial impact of caregiving.
- Advocate for yourself.
- Recognize your emotions. Take a step back, find support, or get help when you need it.
- Take care of yourself. You have to be healthy yourself to continue to provide care for your loved one.
- Utilize caregiving services and support groups.

Additional Resources

There is a wealth of information available online. Here are a few resources to get you started in understanding your loved one's diagnosis:

- **Insight Memory Care Center**
  www.InsightMCC.org or call 703-204-4664

- **Alzheimer's Association**
  www.alz.org

- **Lewy Body Dementia Association**
  www.lbda.org

- **Association for Frontotemporal Degeneration**
  www.theaftd.org

- **SHARE program, by Benjamin Rose Institute**
  http://www.benrose.org/SHARE/INDEX.cfm

CAREGIVING

Caregiving is a long, hard, full time job and caregivers are often called the hidden victims of Alzheimer's disease. Although changes in the brain occur only in the person diagnosed with dementia, changes in behaviors, lifestyle, and demands occur for both the person living with dementia and the caregiver. There is also burden on the caregiver who has to adjust, modify behaviors, and adapt to the effects of the illness and how it presents itself in the person they love.

It can be painful to watch someone you love develop dementia, and some react with denial. A caregiver may not be able to see how bad the person is. While this denial helps decrease the devastating feelings you might have, it may also prevent the caregiver from initiating changes or learning new things that will eventually make caregiving easier.

Sometimes, caregivers are embarrassed by behaviors their loved ones have. This is understandable. It is embarrassing to see your wife walk into a room of company with her nightgown on over her clothes, or have the neighbors bring your husband home after he has slipped out the back door. Unfortunately, these behaviors are a part of the illness, and are just another example of needed adjustments that a caregiver must make.

Why do people do it?

Every caregiver has a different reason for being a caregiver. Some feel obligated and some find themselves caregiving without ever considering whether it is an obligation or a choice. Take a step back, and think of a reason why you have chosen to be a caregiver. Sometimes this perspective can help you remember why you do it.

How do people do it?

In our support groups, caregivers have encouraged others to heed this acronym – QTIP: Quit Taking It Personally. This is certainly easier said than done, especially when caring for someone you're close to such as a spouse or parent. But remember, their behavior isn't a reflection of your relationship; it is most likely a means of communication. It is probably a message of I'm tired, I'm hungry, I don't feel well, I don't understand what's going on, or any other host of concerns. When you're tired or hungry, do you love your spouse any less? No! You're just ready for a nice nap or that steak dinner you've been waiting for all day. Try not to take their actions personally, and remember it's often just a way of communicating needs.

When all else fails, find a little humor in your day. It can be hard to see the glass as half full when your day has started with battles over your loved one getting dressed, not eating breakfast, and refusing their meds. You finally get some clothes on them, and they end up going to the grocery store with you in a polka dot shirt and plaid pants. There are two ways you can handle the situation. You can stomp through the store, trying to get in and out before anyone sees your spouse in such a ridiculous outfit. Or you can remind yourself that your loved one is clean, warm and at least fully dressed, give them their favorite striped hat to wear, and chuckle to yourself about their wonderful (lack of) fashion sense.

What to try:

- Join a support group. There are many other people experiencing similar feelings of loss and embarrassment who will benefit from hearing from you, and you can learn much from them.

- Educate yourself. You can make your caregiving role easier by learning more about the type of dementia you're dealing with.

- Take the time to find a doctor with whom you can work.

- Take breaks (respite) from caregiving right from the start.

- Let other people help you. Assume the offers are sincere and allow others to help. They will stop offering when they get tired of it.

- Create a list of chores or activities you can use assistance with so they can truly be of assistance.

- Consider a respite volunteer as someone to visit with your loved one, while you take some time for yourself.

- Have a family member or friend that can be on stand-by in case you have to step out to deal with another issue.

- Learn to recognize your symptoms of stress and take the time to relieve them.

- Laugh! Some of the situations you find yourself in are downright funny. Consider it a gift and enjoy the humor.

- Take some time for your favorites too – make your favorite side dish with the meal, or add your favorite songs into the playlist so you both have things to enjoy.

- Take care of yourself. Remember, you cannot be an effective caregiver if you fail to stay healthy. Get enough rest, eat right, and exercise regularly to keep your energy up.

- Keep up with your own regular medical checkups. If you do get

1

sick, make sure that you see a health care provider and allow yourself time to recuperate.

- Talk to family, friends and neighbors. Isolation increases stress, so try to call or talk to someone in your circle every day.

- Keep relatives who are not actively involved in caregiving informed of the person's condition. Point them to dementia resources if they seem to ask obscure questions or if they respond inappropriately.

- Plan ahead. Look at adult day health centers, assisted livings, nursing homes, or other places in case you become ill and have to temporarily give up your caregiving responsibilities. Have an alternate plan.

- Ask your loved one about their preferences for care, if able. The SHARE program can help you and your loved one discuss your care preferences and make a plan for future needs.

- Tell neighbors and friends generally about the condition and what they can expect. This will help ease the tension at embarrassing or difficult times.

- There are online and telephone support groups available both locally and nation-wide. These can be a great resource if getting out of the house is tough.

- Consult with specialists. Don't feel like you have to do it all, especially for something not in your skill-set. Contact an elder law attorney, financial planner, aging life care manager, or other professional to help.

FINDING ADDITIONAL CARE

Many caregivers struggle with asking for help. But a crucial part of being a good caregiver is taking good care of yourself. Is the care at home becoming more stressful than it used to be when your loved one was first diagnosed? Ask yourself: Is the help that I'm providing sustainable? For another year or two, or maybe just a month?

Look into options for care. You may not need them until much further down the road — or perhaps never — but it's good to be prepared. It is much easier to do some research now than in the face of an emergency. Tour a few residential facilities nearby, take a look at a day center, or call a couple in-home care agencies to get a sense of what might be the best fit for you and your loved one if or when the need arises.

One of the first questions you'll have to encounter in your search for care is how much care your loved one really needs. Take an honest look at how many activities of daily living they need help with (such as eating, toileting, personal hygiene, dressing, etc.). Does the person have additional medical conditions that need attention (more than just giving a pill once a day)? And how quickly is the person declining?

Keep in mind the person's communication skills as well. Many don't consider how the person will adapt and make friends in their new environment. If your loved one can still communicate and function socially, they will be better able to connect with other participants and staff, increasing their own happiness while also gaining more positive attention from staff who can get to know them.

The step in this process that's often overlooked is how the care is affecting you, the caregiver. Take an honest look at the situation, and be aware of activities you may have already given up in order to take care of your loved one. Ask yourself, are you as active outside of the home as you were previously? How frequently do you feel fatigued? When is the last time you were sick, and did you recover as quickly as usual? If you called a family member or friend for help, are they able to? Are your expectations (actually) realistic? Once you take a look at your situation, talk to a friend or relative you trust, and ask for their honest opinion as well. As one caregiver put it, "The decision is a matter of balance between your loved one's needs and abilities and your own. There is no precisely right time and no perfectly right place. It is an agonizing decision; get all the help you can."

What to try:

- Visit early. You don't want to have to choose a facility in crisis or simply out of the phone book.

- Consider the drive. Is the residential facility too far to visit as much as you'd like? Will it be stressful to take your loved one to a day center in a particular location?

- Check online for questions to ask when touring. Print out a list and take notes when you visit.

- Take a friend with you when visiting if possible. They can be an extra set of eyes and ears.

- Try to visit a care facility when they have a party or special event. You can talk with other families there and gauge their experience.

- Don't be lured into a quick decision by discounts for signing up right away! It's a big decision – and any discount will be negated if you have to move your loved one again.

- Be sure to consider the cost, and what types of payment are accepted.

- Be aware of transfer trauma. Know that your loved one may take time to adjust to the new environment or routine.

- If moving to a residential facility, set up their room beforehand, so they can move into something familiar.

- If starting at a day center, choose a day where there is an activity they would especially enjoy or make sure staff can match them up with a "buddy" with similar interests.

- Give the person time to settle in.

- If the person is resistant to the change, validate their concerns. Take time to listen and help them feel heard.

- Make sure the staff know your loved one's interests so they can engage them right away. Something as simple as knowing how they take their morning coffee helps get the day off on the right foot.

- Ask a trusted friend to visit if it will be upsetting to you or your loved one at first. This can give you peace of mind that your loved one is okay, without causing extra stress.

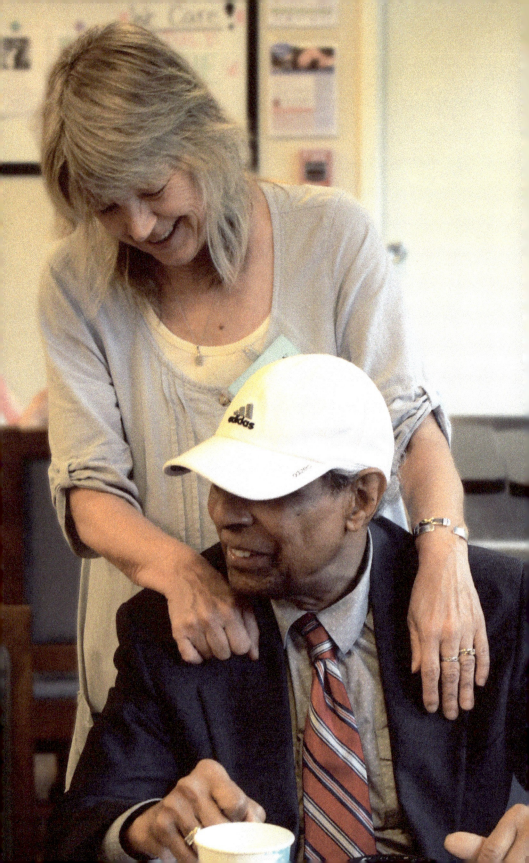

2

ACTIVITIES OF DAILY LIVING

Eating and Mealtime

Sleeping

Bathing and Personal Care

Toileting

From a Family Caregiver

" *I know I'm much stronger in my role as a caregiver. I'm much more nurturing as a spouse because of it.* "

EATING AND MEALTIME

Sharing a meal means more to most people than simple nutrition. Eating is a social event! Who doesn't like to share a great meal with family and friends? Eating is a part of holiday celebrations, family get-togethers and religious occasions, so when life-long eating patterns change due to dementia, caregivers can easily be frustrated. Trying to meet nutritional needs can be challenging enough, while also missing the social needs that sharing meals once filled for both of them.

As eating becomes more difficult, caregivers will need to find alternative ways to meet their own needs for socializing through other family members and friends. During the end stages of the disease, a person with Alzheimer's will lose weight in spite of all the caregiver's efforts at good nutrition. Although it is hard to watch, caregivers need to prepare themselves and realize there is little they can do.

Sometimes the issue of feeding tubes comes up. A flexible straw-like tube may be inserted into the stomach or jejunum (small intestine) from either the nose (through the esophagus) or surgically through the skin on the stomach. Through the tube, nutrition, fluids, and medications can be given when a person can no longer eat. This can be a controversial subject for many caregivers. If at all possible, talk with your loved one before this becomes an issue to gain their perspective on this type of care. Just know there is not one right solution. If you weigh the risks and the benefits and then come to a conclusion, you have made the right choice.

2

Dementia changes:

- Early in the disease, people's judgment regarding food may be impaired; they may think they have eaten when they haven't or vice versa; they may go through a stage of gorging, especially sweets, and gain weight at a rapid rate.

- Later in the disease, people may forget that food served to them is in front of them; they may lose the ability to use silverware or to get the food to their mouths.

- Some will mix food and beverages together, occasionally adding their napkin, and not hesitate to continue eating their concoction.

- Table manners are forgotten, and there are usually more spills with less regard for neatness or order.

- During the later stages of their illness, people are likely to lose their appetite, their ability to eat, and their desire to eat. Some eventually lose the ability to swallow and/or chew food put in their mouths. Choking may become a problem.

- People may not recognize food as food or may think non-food items are edible.

What to try:

- Streamline mealtime so that it's as easy as it can be for you, the caregiver.

- If the person sits with the food in front of them without eating or eats some and then stops, try reminding them that the food is there, or gently tell them to take a bite of something on their plate. They may have forgotten they were in the middle of a meal.

- If it looks like the food is being played with but eating isn't being accomplished, they may be losing their ability to use their silverware. Try making greater use of finger foods; almost anything can be wrapped in a piece of bread and made into a sandwich.

- If cutting food is a problem, cut it in the kitchen and offer it ready to eat on the plate.

- Offer only one utensil at a time if spoon, fork and knife are too confusing.

- Weighted silverware and plates with divided area or lips can be helpful for some people. Products are also available that prevent plates from sliding across the table at meal time.

- Sometimes you just have to help a person get started by holding the hand on the spoon, putting the spoon in the potatoes, and helping get it to the mouth. Once or twice with you doing it and the person may continue by themselves.

- If people mix their food, offer only one item on the plate at a time and hold the liquids until they are finished eating. Limit access to condiments as they may be applied too liberally or just add another layer of confusion.

- Don't fill cups too full and only serve food and beverages at moderate temperatures. People may burn their mouth and throat before they realize the food/drink is too hot for them; they probably won't wait for it to cool down.

- If the person is in a gorging mode, remove sweets from the house but have plenty of nutritious snack foods on hand (carrot sticks, apples, granola bars, etc). Realize that you won't be able to satisfy the person's urge to eat, but you can offer healthy alternatives.

- During this phase, people may lose their manners and may eat off other people's plates, or eat non-food items. Occasionally the urge to eat is overwhelming and the person may choke trying to eat too quickly.

2

- Learn how to do the Heimlich maneuver in case a person chokes.

- If you have to feed the person, try to do it in a matter of fact manner and slowly. You may want to have a book to read or a recording to listen to in between mouthfuls since it can take a long time to chew up food and swallow it. Don't try to force a person to eat, teeth can break and lips and gums can get injured.

- Soft foods and those easier to chew and swallow are often more acceptable than items requiring much chewing. Make liberal use of the blender and food processor, to minimize the need for chewing and to facilitate swallowing.

- If a person seems to be able to chew the food but not swallow, sometimes stroking the neck can help initiate the process.

- Difficulty swallowing may be a temporary condition. Many caregivers have gotten through this by giving thickened liquids during this phase. Milk shakes, pudding, ice cream, hot cereals, and sherbet can be swallowed more easily than watery liquids or foods that require a two-step process of chewing, then swallowing. Thick soups are nutritious and relatively easy to eat and swallow. Ask the doctor or nutritionist about thickening agents that can even turn water into "pudding" consistency.

- People at some stages may refuse to eat, or be unable to eat. Caregivers need to think about this and talk over the options with their doctor and the members of their support group and family.

- Unless the doctor has told you to limit fluids, try to offer water, fruit juices and other clear liquids frequently. If night-time wetting is a problem, limit them in the early evening. Try using straws for neater, more ample intake of liquids.

- Check with your doctor about giving the person alcoholic beverages. Some medications don't mix well with alcohol, while some people have a calm relaxed evening after they have had a glass of wine before or with dinner.

SLEEPING

Nighttime should be for sleeping. As a caregiver, you've put in a long hard day, and you need your beauty sleep to replenish for the next one. Unfortunately, the person with dementia may not share this view!

Be prepared that during some parts of the disease process nighttime may be worse than daytime. Confusion may increase, as well as incontinence, and feelings of loneliness or being afraid. Nighttime wakefulness can be particularly hard on the caregiver, especially if you are caregiving alone. And, of course, not getting enough sleep yourself only makes the caregiving during the day harder! Nighttime waking may be a phase for some individuals, so you may need to consider asking for additional help, or hiring a nighttime care aide.

Dementia changes:

With decreased input from the senses, the failing brain is more likely to misinterpret stimuli in the environment. A dark blanket in a dimly lit corner may look more like a big animal. Voices on the TV may be misinterpreted as someone trying to talk to the person. Other changes include:

- Some people simply can't remember that the caregiver is sleeping in the next room (or bed!) and feel afraid being all alone.

- Sometimes a person may awaken to go to the toilet and then not be able to find the bedroom or bed upon return.

- Sometimes a person will stay up all night and then sleep during the day, changing nights into days.

- Sometimes people experience changes in behaviors and restlessness as the sun goes down (sundowning).

- During a hypermotor phase in the course of a memory impairment, a person may be very tired but be unable to lie down long enough to fall asleep (not all people experience this).

What to try:

- Work towards a peaceful evening. To reduce sundowning, keep your demands low and keep environment well lit, at least until bed time.

- Limit fluids in the evenings. Don't serve caffeinated drinks and avoid exercise. Strenuous activities are known to cause increased agitation or excitement in the evening.

- Establish a daytime routine that does not include a lot of naps. If the person has already reversed the day/night schedule, it may take some concentrated effort and some outside help to reverse the sleep/wake cycle, but it can be done. Adult day health centers often provide the necessary stimuli to keep the person awake.

- Leave a rather bright light on in the person's room so surroundings can be recognized upon awakening. This light doesn't need to be directly on the person as it may impede sleep.

- Warm milk contains tryptophan, a natural substance which induces sleep.

- Sedation is a side effect of some medications and can be used to the patient's advantage if taken before bed. Talk with your loved one's doctor about the best time to take certain medications.

- Sometimes sleep-inducing medications help, but not always.

Some produce such a hangover effect that a person cannot function the day after taking the medicine.

- Life has been made bearable for some folks by hiring a nighttime companion who can be up with the person while the caregiver sleeps. For others, short-term respite on a regular basis gives the caregiver a chance to revive drooping spirits and catch up on sleep during the day.

- Buy an inexpensive nighttime bedside monitor so that you can rest assured of your loved one's safety during the night.

- Relax a little. If the person gets up, changes back into clothes at midnight and then falls asleep on the bed or in a chair, let it be. Do not insist that the person wear pajamas or sleep in bed if sleeping in the chair is comfortable.

- If sleep problems persist, you may want to consult with your physician to rule out other problems that could be affecting your loved one's sleep.

2

BATHING & PERSONAL CARE

It may be difficult and unpleasant to see someone neglect grooming, cleanliness, and personal appearance. You may find yourself angry with the person who also refuses your offers of assistance, embarrassed about how your loved one appears to others, frustrated by irrational claims like: "I just had a bath this morning" or "these are clean clothes," or falsely thinking the person's lack of cleanliness is a reflection on you.

Set realistic goals that balance an acceptable level of cleanliness with the hassle factor involved. Work on accepting that some bathing is better than no bathing at all!

Dementia changes:

Many people with dementia go through a phase when they seem to be terrified of bathing or showering. They might misinterpret requests to remove clothes or have a terrible time admitting that they need help with this process. People with dementia may have trouble:

- Remembering to change clothes or to bathe.

- Completing the complex task of bathing (a series of simple tasks that must be completed in specific order).

- Performing the motor tasks necessary to complete a bath.

- Realizing their need for assistance.

- Remembering or accomplishing tooth-brushing, hair care, or shaving.

What to try:

- Identify the person's usual bath time and routine; you'll probably have more success if you continue this pattern. Write bath times on the weekly calendar as a visual reminder.

- Try to break the task down into small steps and talk the person through: "here's the wash cloth, wash your face."

- Don't announce that it's "bath time" if you know you're going to get a negative response. Instead, get everything ready and invite the person to the bathroom, be friendly, guiding, and directive in approach.

- Arrange a "reward" after bathing (e.g. having a cup of tea and cookies) to soothe and replace frustrating bath time feelings.

- Try a bath chair or bench (available in home health stores) and a hand held shower nozzle. This may be less frightening than immersion in a tub or having water sprayed from a stationary shower head.

- Put nonskid strips on the tub floor and attach a grip bar to the tub for safety. Don't use bath oil and keep radios, hair dryers, and electrical equipment out of reach. Wipe up splashes on the floor so people won't fall.

- Assure privacy and make sure the bathroom is warm enough.

- Encourage the person to do as much as possible to increase feelings of self-esteem and confidence.

- Approach the bath matter-of-factly and avoid whispering or using infantile words as these will increase discomfort and embarrassment.

- If you can't get the person in the tub/shower (spouses sometimes bathe together), give a "sponge bath." This can be done while the person is sitting on the toilet or standing at the sink.

- Gender of person who is helping may make a difference in the person's acceptance of help. You may need to call on a niece, son or enlist a "bather" from a home care agency.

- Utilize beauty/barber shops for hair care (one less task for you and most people with dementia enjoy being "pampered" in this way).

- Try fluoride or other sponge swabs for oral hygiene if a toothbrush is refused.

- Electric tooth brushes and shavers may be easier to use when you have to take over these tasks for the person. Introducing them while the person is able to adapt may lessen resistance and/or fear later on.

- If all else fails, try products that may provide "waterless" baths (such as hand sanitizer gels and dry shampoos).

2

TOILETING

It's hard to watch someone you love lose the ability to regulate urination and defecation. It can often be embarrassing for both you and the person with dementia. Privacy itself may be the greater issue since these functions are almost always done alone.

Dementia changes:

Changes caused by the progression of the disease may include:

- Messages that the bladder needs to be emptied may be recognized too late or slow response to these stimuli may cause persons to be incontinent.

- Persons may forget where the toilet is located.

- Persons may void in inappropriate places, misperceived to be toilets/urinals (e.g. sinks, flower pots, trash cans, corners).

- Persons may lose the ability to remove clothes for toileting.

- Persons may go to the bathroom frequently out of fear of soiling themselves.

- Some medications may cause or increase incontinence.

- Nighttime incontinence (nocturia) may be related to a physical condition or may be the result of increased confusion because of darkness or dim lighting, or the onset of nighttime wandering.

- True incontinence related to dementia decline usually occurs late in the illness.

What to try:

- Use a matter-of-fact approach with toileting issues.

- Use adult words that are familiar to the person; give clear direct messages (don't whisper or use baby talk regarding toileting issues since this can increase embarrassment).

- There are several brands of incontinence products (briefs, undergarments, shields) in different styles for different kinds of incontinence. Check with pharmacies or members of a support group to get advice on what to try and where to find them. Begin making use of these products at first signs of serious soiling or incontinence, especially at night.

- Try to figure out why the person is soiling themselves. Can't find the bathroom? Show them where it is or put a picture on the door. Can't find the toilet? Put a bright colored rug on the floor at the toilet so it stands out. Can't undo clothes? Give help or simplify their clothing.

- Does the person go to the toilet frequently (more than once every hour and a half)? Check with doctor to rule out urinary tract infection (UTI). UTI's may cause a person to be even more confused or agitated. The person may not feel burning or have other common symptoms of a urinary tract infection. Incontinence or frequent toilet trips may be your only clue (Urine may turn very dark, cloudy and have a strong, foul odor).

- Has an accident on the way to the bathroom? Take the person at regular intervals (One person may need to go every one and a half hours, another may stay dry for three or four hours before needing to go).

- Soils at night? Give plenty of fluids during day but stop fluid intake after a few hours before bedtime.

- If wetting occurs at the same time every night, set alarm for a half hour before, get up and take the person to the bathroom. This may or may not be effective but is worth a try.

- Wets in hallway/bedroom – everywhere but toilet at night? Make sure bathroom is well lit and the door stays opened. Tie the door handle to the towel rack or use door stop if you need to. Some people close the door after using the bathroom and then can't find it when they need it again. Make sure the bathroom door can be opened from the outside, in case the person using it locks them self in.

- Portable toilet chairs or commodes can be placed near the person's bed.

- Keep all soiled material – linens, bed and chair pads - in tightly closed containers until they can be discarded or washed. Wash the person well after an incontinent episode to reduce odor and prevent skin break down.

- Cover mattress with a plastic cover (large trash-bags work well) to prevent urine from soaking in.

- Consider removing rugs or carpeting on frequently-wetted spots.

- If incontinence begins all of a sudden, report it to the physician; it could be a sign of a physical problem or a side effect of a medication.

- Run water in the sink or flush the toilet to stimulate urination.

- If resistance is encountered in toileting, try to develop a "bear hug" procedure in which the caregiver can remove loose fitting clothing and guide the person to sit on the toilet all in one operation. The disarming affection enables this to work regularly.

COMMUNICATION & BEHAVIORS

Communication

Troublesome Behaviors

Hostility and Aggression

Wandering

From a Family Caregiver

" *When you find the right strategy that helps them, it just does so much for your peace of mind, and your quality of life. When Mom is happy, I'm happy – and that's what Insight has done for us.* "

COMMUNICATION

Being able to talk to a person is the basis for all of our relationships in life. When the communication system breaks down, troubles add up.

To understand how to best communicate with someone with dementia, you need to understand the basics of the disease, and how it might be affecting the person. Common behaviors in all dementias include progressive memory loss, language problems, poor judgment and reasoning, difficulty with impulse control, and poor coping skills. All of these make the person more emotional, and can easily lead to increased frustration. Imagine yourself in a foreign country – how do you feel if you can't follow a conversation or can't find the right words to say? Think of things from their perspective, and understanding communication will immediately be easier.

In the early stages of a person's illness, utilize their ability to communicate with you and talk about what is going on! As the disease progresses, you as the caregiver are going to have to make some hard choices and it will be much easier if you discuss the issues together.

Although there are techniques that can help ease the problem of more difficult or lost communication, there is still likely to be a feeling of loss for that person and the communication you once shared. Try to recognize that some of your anger is based on grief and try not to direct this anger at the person.

3

Talking and singing use the same muscles that eating and swallowing do. Listening even though you may not be able to understand what is said shows respect and compassion. So, even when things are not making perfect sense, talking and active listening are important.

Communication is 7% verbal (words and their meanings), 55% voice (pitch, tone, tempo, volume), and 38% body language (facial expressions, eyes, posture, movements, gestures). This is important because people with dementia may no longer understand the meaning of the words but they will be able to understand the remaining 93% of your communication. Make sure your body and voice are conveying the same message your words are trying to convey.

Dementia changes:

Language is usually affected early in the disease and communication becomes harder as time goes by. Problems occur throughout the process and include:

- Not recognizing a word or a phrase almost as if it were spoken in a foreign language.

- Not being able to name things (noun finding), eventually not being able to say any words in a coherent fashion.

- "Perseveration" – repeating words or phrases without being able to continue to express the rest of the thought.

- Misnaming objects or people…but getting close (some may say mother when they mean wife, or pencil for paper. This can make it difficult to determine if the person doesn't know the difference between wife and mother or if they are saying the wrong word).

- A tendency for non-native English speakers to return to their language of childhood or combine languages with little insight into which language they are speaking at the time.

- Eventual loss of ability to communicate with others.

Remember – understanding what is being said often outlasts the ability to speak appropriately!

What to try:

- Assume the person understands everything that you are saying.
- Nobody likes to be talked about, so include the person in your conversation; or wait until he/she is not around if you need to say something that may be upsetting.
- Get the person's attention before you start talking.
- Establish eye contact before making any physical contact with the person.
- Use a gentle touch.
- Call the person by name.
- Deliver your message using short, simple words.
- Keep communication on an adult-to-adult level. Avoid baby talk or demeaning expressions.
- Smile, and shake the person's hand so that he/she knows you are approaching them as an adult.
- S-p-e-a-k s-l-o-w-l-y (expanded speech).
- Give only one message at a time.
- If your voice is high, try lowering the pitch; don't shout.
- Limit choices. If it's time for lunch, don't ask the person if he/she is ready to eat; just say, "It's time to eat." On the other hand, give the person choices when it's okay: "Would you like coffee or tea?"

3

- If this is still challenging, stick to yes or no questions: "Would you like some tea?"

- Watch your body language: if you are angry, your face or gestures may show it, even if your words are sweet.

- Help the people put words to their thoughts if you know what they are trying to say, e.g. "You're trying to ask when your wife is coming, aren't you?"

- Ask uncomplicated questions one at a time, and repeat them, using the same words, if the person doesn't respond. Just make sure to give them time to respond!

- Listen for a response. It may take up to ninety seconds for the person to figure out what you've said and come up with the right words in response.

- Use non-controlling, non-confronting statements.

- Try to agree with at least part of what the person is saying. Don't start every answer with "No, you can't!" For example, say "Could you please come here" rather than "No, don't go out the door!" or "You're right, you are going home right after lunch", is easier to take than "You have a long time to wait."

- Change the subject rather than waste energy arguing. It's impossible to have a rational argument with someone who can't be rational. Instead, compliment them on their smile or ask for their help, this may derail their argumentative attempts and help you feel like you're still in charge.

- Avoid questions that rely on memory. Don't ask, "don't you remember the time that…", but rather say, "I was thinking about the time that…" and tell the story and allow them to respond from there.

- A great phrase to use? "Tell me about it."

- Join the individual where they are, rather than dragging them into your reality. What's not helpful: "Well your parents sold that house 20 years ago and now it's a shopping mall!" More helpful: "Your mom always used to have the prettiest flowers on the front porch at home."

- A simple written note can sometimes help to calm a person who is trying to remember a particular piece of information.

- Tell the person that everything is going according to plan.

- Although it often seems like a waste of time, it's important to keep on talking even when you are sure you aren't getting through. Explain what you're doing, update the person on familiar events, and use your gift of gab in an attempt to stay in touch with your loved one.

- Reduce background noise if possible. Although you can hear over the radio or other's conversations, the person with Alzheimer's probably can't.

3

TROUBLESOME BEHAVIORS

When you think you've seen it all, another behavior that seems worse than all the rest may appear. It is important to keep in mind that Alzheimer's is an ever changing presentation of behaviors reflecting internal deterioration of brain cells. As more cells die, behaviors will change. It sometimes helps to know that a particular behavior will probably last only six to nine months. It helps to see the light at the end of the tunnel. It also helps to know that you are not the only one dealing with "bad" behaviors. Try and find out from others how they have handled them. Not everyone who has dementia will develop these behaviors.

3

For better or for worse, caregivers must be aware that most behavior traits will change over time. Some will disappear entirely, but others will commence with no predictability. When a caregiver encounters a new aspect of behavior, remember the common support group reminder: "This, too, will change."

People who are coming to grips with a diagnosis of dementia, or even those who have limited awareness that something has changed, will react to this change. Some people become very depressed; others may become very angry and frustrated. Sometimes, even before it is diagnosed, the person with dementia may become very suspicious and distrusting - especially of the caregiver. If something is missing the person with dementia may think it has been stolen or worse, that the caregiver has hidden it. This distrust often leads to anger directed at the caregiver which is often hard to dissipate. Later on, people with dementia may do things that are annoying to the caregiver (for example, someone might disassemble a photo album you have just completed). You won't be able to medicate this kind of behavior away and you may not be able to change it.

Ask yourself these questions:
- Are they trying to communicate something with the behavior?

- Is the behavior detrimental to them or others?

- Does it cause me, the caregiver, any more work?

If you answer "no" to all three of these questions, don't spend any energy trying to change the behavior. Leave it be. Spend your energy focusing on ways to distract yourself and/or lessen the annoyance you are feeling.

Repetitive phrases: "I want to go home… I want to go home…" This phrase or a similar one may be repeated thousands of times during a day, even when the person is at home. Picking at clothes, smoothing things out, tearing paper into tiny shreds, collecting papers or assorted unrelated objects (which then become treasures), rearranging items on counters or in drawers, rubbing hands or head, clapping, whistling, singing, making grimacing facial expressions, and grinding teeth are a few of the behaviors that sometimes develop in the middle to late stages of the disease.

Remember, the person with dementia cannot change their behaviors. YOU must change your response to the situation.

Start with the 6 Ws:
- What is happening?

- Why is the behavior happening?

- Who is involved?

- Where does the behavior happen?

- When does the behavior usually happen?

- What next?

These questions might help identify triggers before the behavior happens. But most likely, you'll have to ask – what next?

- You can ignore the behavior, if it's not hurting anyone (maybe it's just annoying!).

- You can reinforce or support by validating their emotions.

- You can redirect the behavior and re-engage the person based on their personal interests and favorite things.

What to try:

- Make sure that the person is not in pain, sitting on something uncomfortable or too long in one position, that clothes and/or shoes are not ill-fitting or that he is not constipated or needing to urinate. Any of these things can make a usually quiet person more vocal or restless.

- If you are confident that you have met the person's needs and the behavior still persists, you must move on to survival techniques. Although these behaviors are very annoying to caregivers, the person may be completely unaware that it is coming from them and may not be able to control it. This is one area in particular to use your imagination and creativity. Listed below are things that have worked once in a while and deserve a try.

  - "Gum Therapy" – If the person can chew and swallow easily, try giving gum to chew so there is something in the mouth. Rarely will a person call out when their mouth is filled. Be sure to use gum that won't stick to dentures.

3

- "Cereal Therapy" – Give the person a non-breakable bowl of dry cereal to eat. It has lots of fiber and won't significantly add to caloric intake.

- Keep important mail and documents locked up, out of sight and out of reach. Remember that these papers are very important to the person and need to be treated accordingly while the person is interested in them. If it's time to take them away, say, "Let me take care of those for you," rather than: "okay, put that mess in the trash and quit playing!" Sometimes the mere motion of going through things makes them feel better.

- If a person insists on reorganizing papers, folding them and sticking them away, keep a basket of flyers, ads, or playing cards that are not important to you and can be sorted.

- When the person is accusing the caregiver of hiding or taking something, try not to react defensively; instead say, "I know you're worried about your purse (or whatever is missing). I love you, and I'll help you look for it."

- Check, however superficially, all trash cans before emptying. They may contain valuables put there by the person "for safe keeping." Check your garbage disposal units before using.

- Try putting headphones on the person with favorite music to try to calm agitation or anxiety, or play familiar songs in the room.

- If the house is big enough, arrange a safe place for the person where yelling will not disturb the rest of the family. Check on the person regularly and leave them be. Many people waste energy and time trying to get a loud person to be quiet with no results.

- Occasionally medications can be tried. A consultation with your doctor or a geropsychiatrist can be very helpful to determine if medications may be helpful for your loved one's current situation.

HOSTILITY AND AGGRESSION

Avoiding a crisis is much better than having to get through one. Caregiving is so frustrating sometimes that it becomes easy to enter into the cycle of aggression.

It is also very easy to blame yourself for not being patient enough... not trying harder... not being a "super-person" – able to do all things for everyone calmly and correctly each and every time. And then there's guilt – "the gift that keeps on giving;" even after the person with dementia has long since forgotten what the argument was about, you're left feeling angry and guilty. Look at the aggression cycle; see if you can figure out the events leading up to the outbreak, and what you could do differently the next time. Review communication skills, since this is where many aggressive outbreaks begin. Then, take a deep slow breath, maybe two, and think about something that makes you laugh. These events have happened before and will happen again. They are a part of caregiving.

Relationships aren't perfect, and how you felt about each other before will definitely influence the caregiving scenario. Children who become the primary caregiver of their parents may feel like the parents are a burden. Children may resent responsibility for caregiving for both older parents and their own children.

If you find yourself so angry that you are afraid you will actually hurt someone, you are getting a very strong signal that you need respite or more help with your caregiving duties. Recognizing your own caregiving limit is very positive. Don't allow yourself to get boxed in to an "either – or" situation, there are always other possibilities.

3

Angry feelings are normal; behaving in a negative way in response to these feelings means you need help. Get help.

Dementia changes:

A person with dementia may have very little insight into their illness and not understand why there are limitations on activities ("What do you mean I can't drive the car? I've been driving the car since I was 14!"). As the disease progresses these changes may occur:

- Impaired judgment combined with memory loss and decreased abilities to carry out simple motor tasks can result in unsafe situations.

- Frustration with the continual parade of losses that a person with Alzheimer's disease has to accept can make even the meekest person lose control or give up in despair.

- A noisy, crowded or visually active environment can contribute to an explosive situation.

- Although verbal skills may deteriorate, many people with dementia pick up on caregiver's moods and feelings. If the caregiver is upset, the person with dementia may become upset more easily.

- Validate the person's emotions, "I see you are feeling frustrated. How can I help?"

- Do not argue or correct.

What to try:

- Always explain what you are going to do before you do it.

- Use distractions; talk about something totally off the subject.

- Ask the person to help and try to give the appearance of involvement, even if it is difficult to get an opinion on a particular matter.

- If at first the person says no, take a deep breath, walk away, come back in 2 or 3 minutes and try again as if it were the first time. It often works the second time around.

- Change face. If there is someone else around who can ask the person to do something, have them try.

- Always leave an exit route for yourself if you think you are in physical danger.

- Remember this safety hierarchy:

  1. Protect yourself from harm first – you cannot be effective if you are injured or cornered.

  2. Protect the person with dementia.

  3. Protect physical belongings. (In other words, don't risk your safety or your loved one's safety to protect a document or a piece of furniture).

  4. Call 911 if you, or your family member, are at risk.

Some of the things that "trigger" an aggressive crisis are obvious, but in many cases the trigger is more obscure.

3

Obvious Triggers

- Misunderstanding a question
- Inability to find the right word to express a thought
- Too high expectations by caregiver/not enough guidance
- Change from routine
- Change in medication
- Change in diet
- Frustration in not being able to complete a task
- Too much stimulation

Obscure Triggers

- Falling barometer
- Change in lighting (dusk and dawn)
- Increased background noise
- Caregiver moving too rapidly
- Introduction of new people
- Physical pain that caregiver is not aware of
- Temperature- room is too cold or too hot
- Television (disturbing news events or images)
- Infections
- Crowded rooms

WANDERING

Wandering by a person with dementia can be very stressful to the caregiver. You may find yourself worrying about the person getting lost or hurt, feeling trapped or locked inside your own home, tired of watching the person constantly "on the go," frustrated by how clever a person can be about getting out or how fast they can move, or sure that your loved one will never walk away because they never have.

Do the best you can to keep the person safe and have a plan in place if they do get lost. National programs such as the Alzheimer's Association's Safe Return program or Project Lifesaver are good options to include in your plan. GPS devices are also becoming more popular and widely available. There are many types designed specifically for those with dementia, including shoe inserts, keychain, pendant, or pocket devices, or you can even consider a generic fitness tracker band. These products have options for you to monitor your loved one yourself, or connect with subscription services for 24/7 alert monitoring.

The caregiver has to decide how much "freedom" a person with Alzheimer's disease should have. At some point the person's need to be safe will outweigh their diminished ability to decide where they want to go and when. As the skills to remember landmarks or right from left diminish, the caregiver will have to become more involved in ensuring the person's safety and limiting unaccompanied walks.

Expect that being in an unfamiliar location might exacerbate wandering and be ready to secure all new environments.

3

Dementia changes:

Sometimes people with dementia like to walk because it is one of the few things they can still do without having their losses show. However, wandering can become a problem. Some people with Alzheimer's go through a hyper-motor stage (that usually lasts for 6 to 9 months) when they are constantly on the move. People with dementia may have trouble:

- Recognizing familiar landmarks.

- Keeping a sense of direction.

- Recognizing an object as different from its background (e.g., "seeing" a chair in front of a wall).

- Understanding time/distance issues (e.g., wishing to return to a home that no longer exists).

- Remembering their destination.

- Losing visual recognition as they move past objects.

What to try:

- Sign your loved one up for a national wandering prevention program, such as the Alzheimer's Association's Safe Return or Project Lifesaver.

- Consider a GPS tracking device to help locate the person.

- Make a plan of steps to take if the person gets lost or falls.

- Keep and update all emergency information.

- Inform your neighbors about the possibility of wandering and give them specific instructions about what to do.

- Accept the fact that verbal instructions to stay put are unreliable.

- Provide a safe wandering space if possible.

- Take supervised walks and include exercise in their daily routine.

- Dress your loved one in bright clothing, especially if you'll be somewhere you need to find them in a crowd.

- Try "sock therapy." A person who normally wears shoes outside may not leave if they are in just socks. Put the shoes out of sight.

- Try to keep ID on the person. They may not always have a wallet on them, but consider other options like medical ID jewelry or sewing their name and contact information into their jacket.

- Hang bells on doorknobs to alert you to opening of taboo doors.

- Install locks that open by key on the inside of the door, wear the key yourself or hang it hidden from view.

- Place locks in unusual places (high or low on doors).

- Use child-resistant knob covers on doorknobs.

- For those in the earlier stages, try a "Do Not Enter" sign on the door. Alternatively, try adding signs with words or pictures for doors your loved one uses often (bedroom, bathroom), so they don't wander out the front door when looking for the bathroom.

- If they leave their "safety zone" and you try to get them back:

  - Do ask for their help to do something.

  - Do acknowledge their verbal message about their plan.

  - Do provide correct information if it helps.

  - Do fall in step and walk with the person for a short while and then suggest going "inside" for a reason.

  - Do not say "stay here" or "don't go" or other blatantly controlling statements.

  - Do not physically pull on the person unless there is acute danger of physical injury.

ACTIVITIES

Activities...What to Do Between Meals

Tips for Travel

From a Family Caregiver

" *Insight really meets participants where they're at, and engages them with all the things they can still do and love.* "

ACTIVITIES...WHAT TO DO BETWEEN MEALS

It is really hard to watch a once active person "do nothing" or misuse familiar tools or household objects. However, when a caregiver can provide appropriate activities, they can help restore motor, social, and cognitive functioning, build confidence, and develop coping skills. While it may seem very overwhelming to fill your loved one's day, many simplified activities can still help the person feel useful and productive.

It is easy for the caregiver to equate the loss of abilities with a return to childhood. The person is no longer capable of complex games or enjoying usual types of grown-up entertainment. Simplifying favorite activities is the best place to start, however, caregivers must be mindful that children's formats may insult an older adult who is still capable of understanding what they see.

4

- Help the person feel useful and still be part of the family.

- Recognize and capitalize on remaining strengths.

- Provide meaningful activities that they enjoy and can still do.

- Accept the fact that many activities may require your supervision or assistance.

Dementia changes:

- "Apraxia," the loss of ability to do routine motor activities, which frequently occurs in the middle stages of Alzheimer's, prevents a person from completing even the easiest of motor skills. Thus, even cutting in a straight line can become very challenging.

- A person may still have awareness and realize that craft or work products have deteriorated and thus he will not attempt to make them. They may resist the activity without trying to simplify the steps.

- Work or activities that depend on a process of steps in order are often difficult, or not able to be completed.

- Attention span may be greatly reduced for independent activities. During a hyper-motor phase (when a person becomes restless and active), it may be very difficult to help the person focus on anything for any length of time.

- Social skills may long outlast a person's other abilities. The person may do nothing for the caregiver and yet be very cooperative with another relative or unfamiliar person.

What to try:

- In the beginning, carrying out normal routines may keep the person active but, as the disease progresses (and the person gives up bookkeeping or pleasure reading) other activities can be substituted.

- Try to focus on the person's remaining skills, even if they may seem minimal.

- Your attitude will be important in determining how the person views an activity. If you see it as a "time filler," the person is likely to reject it and see it as useless.

- Including the person verbally in your tasks may work well. Tell the person what you are doing and comment on it. Ask questions about how they like doing similar activities.

- Humor and the ability to laugh and dance (or sway with music) are very powerful ways to help people feel better. Finding ways to incorporate these into both of your lives will help lighten your burden. It may be the last thing you want to do, but best thing you can do!

- If a person comes up with an activity he seems to enjoy and it is safe, inexpensive, and keeps them occupied, encourage them to continue it even if it seems meaningless to you!

- Participating in an Adult Day Center with their peers goes a long way toward meeting the needs for companionship and a sense of purpose for persons with dementia. Being able to participate in a daily routine and activities on their level can prove useful and comforting. Contact the National Association of Adult Day Services for help finding an adult day program in your area (www.nadsa.org).

Ideas for Activities:

Cognitive Activities

Cognitive activities access long-term memory (memory from the past) and help maintain skills.

- Cognitive activities could include: crossword puzzles, word finds, jigsaw puzzles, solving math problems, and playing games like chess, checkers, Uno, gin rummy, bridge. These can be adjusted to the person's abilities but must be somewhat challenging.

- If these activities become too challenging, try a puzzle with fewer pieces, or make up simpler rules to the game (just match colors of Uno cards, sort playing cards by suit, etc.)

- Even after people have lost their ability to comprehend, they may enjoy the act of looking at a newspaper or thumbing through magazines.

4

- Discussions, based on a hobby, interest, or news (current, seasonal, or historical).

- Reminiscing can easily access long-term memory. Talk about a favorite memory from the current season (summer vacations, going back to school, holiday traditions, etc).

Physical Activities

Physical activities aim to maintain and improve strength, flexibility, balance, movement and endurance.

- Exercise is good for the person with dementia and the caregiver. Walking is a great way to relive stress and work off excess energy. It is also an activity that a person with dementia may do without any disabilities showing.

- Dance (even just in the living room!).

- Stretching exercises; chair exercises can also be used for arm and leg stretching.

- Active games, such as balloon toss or corn hole can be fun for both of you.

- Some may enjoy Wii fitness games such as bowling, tennis or golf, especially if real versions have become too difficult.

Social Activities

Social activities are more than just fun! They build positive relationships and provide opportunity for expression.

- Socializing is an activity! Try to get out to see friends and family, or have them come to you. Engaging in conversation is a great way to stay mentally active.

- If you can't get out to see family, consider a Skype or Facetime call. Your loved one may connect better seeing the person than just talking on the phone.

- Make an outing to a local park or museum.

- Try out an arts or crafts project (and remember the process is more important than the outcome!).

- If they're not up for creating art, games like Pictionary can be a creative alternative.

- Videos, either oldies that the person may have seen a million times, nature films or wildlife documentaries may move slowly enough for a person to enjoy watching with you. It can also then be a topic of conversation over dinner.

Sensory Activities

These activities aim to stimulate all of the senses, to engage a passive individual, or calm someone who is agitated.

- Listen to a favorite song or album.

- Try a hand or foot massage.

- Tactile items can be engaging, and can be something as simple as a silky scarf, or fuzzy earmuffs.

- Bake a favorite dessert (enjoy the smells and tastes!).

- Flip through a coffee table book or a picture book of art, travel photos, or another interest.

4

Spiritual Activities

Spiritual activities provide a sense of healing and comfort.

- Sing favorite hymns. Many will remember carols or church songs.

- Do a morning prayer together.

- Yoga, Tai Chi or other stretching can be calming.

- Listen to a favorite gospel choir.

- Watch or listen to a church service online if getting out is difficult.

Expressive Activities

Creativity provides an opportunity for expression, especially as word-finding becomes difficult.

- Try an adult coloring book.

- Try to copy or imitate a favorite painting.

- Write a short story or poem together.

- Do Mad-Libs together (or make up your own!).

- Build something out of blocks, dominoes, or make a card house.

- Make cards to send to friends or family.

- Arts and crafts can be difficult depending on the person. Keep in mind that the process is more important than the product and often joint projects where you do the complex parts and the person does the sanding or the cutting may be more acceptable.

Help Around the House

Sometimes you just need to get a little work done! Your loved one can still try to help, and more importantly, feel useful in the process.

- Break down household tasks into simple steps; for instance, you put the place mats on the table, hand the person the spoons to put one on each mat, and then give them the forks, etc.

- Things that involve repetition of the same motor skills can be satisfying. Activities like folding towels and stuffing envelopes, dusting, raking or sweeping seem to work well.

- Remember that the quality of the job may not be as good as you yourself could do. Thank the person for their help and know that you may have to redo the task later.

TIPS FOR TRAVEL

We all need a vacation once in a while. A vacation from work, a vacation from home, or just a trip to see something new! And you probably have fond memories of a favorite trip – perhaps a road trip as a child, an exotic honeymoon, or a favorite weekend retreat. A diagnosis of dementia can take the "vacation" out of vacation planning – but travel is certainly not impossible. Whether you're planning a day trip to visit family or a cross-country excursion, there are ways to minimize the anxiety, and allow everyone to enjoy the vacation.

Most importantly, plan ahead and be realistic. Take time in advance to plan out the trip. Remember, people with memory impairment respond to their environment, so if you end up stressed out when you can't find the hotel, more than likely, they will pick up on your stress and start exhibiting signs of stress and anxiety themselves.

Understand that you may not get to everything you have planned – and that's okay! A nice afternoon nap back at the hotel or sitting down for a cup of coffee at the local coffee shop can be just as enjoyable. Have a back-up plan if an activity isn't going well, or just take a break. Everyone will have more fun, whether you hit one site on the list or all ten. And isn't that the whole point of vacation?

4

Dementia Changes:

- Confusion may increase when out of the daily routine.

- Your loved one might be more prone to wander and get lost in unfamiliar areas. Even a simple trip to a nearby restroom could be difficult.

- Because dementia reduces one's ability to plan, prioritize, and make decisions, your loved one might not be much help when preparing for the trip or when decisions need to be made. Decisions that need to be made "on the spot" are likely to be particularly difficult and may create anxiety.

- Changes in mood and behavior can occur when traveling. For example, your loved one might be more withdrawn, more agitated, or less socially appropriate (e.g., less inhibited).

- Given their memory impairment, they may be more prone to ask you the same questions repeatedly ("Where are we going?" "What are we doing today?")

- Traveling can be tiring for anyone but can be exhausting for people with cognitive difficulties.

Things to try:

- As much as possible, try to stick to the person's familiar routine. Have dinner around the same time, take naps and go to bed around the same time.

- Keep the personal care routine the same too – if they always take a shower before bed, make sure that's in the plan.

- Plan travel around your normal sleeping routine as well. Pick flights that get you in before bedtime (or sundowning), or take breaks from a long drive.

- Make extra copies of IDs and any important travel documents to keep in your suitcase in case your loved one misplaces theirs.

- Create a quick flyer with your loved ones information and a recent picture. Then if you get separated you can easily hand this to gate attendants or security.

- If you're staying in a hotel, try to reserve a quieter room at the end of the hall, versus near the elevators or ice machine.

- Make a list of any and all medications, including the name, dose, and frequency to help you stay on schedule.

- Consider packing medications in a carry-on bag, in case there is a delay in getting your checked luggage.

- Don't be afraid to use sheet protectors for your important documents or lists to avoid getting them wet – especially if you're going to the beach!

SAFETY

Home Safety

Giving up the Keys

Medication Guide

From a Family Caregiver

" *In all honesty we could not have gotten through this dementia journey without Insight.* "

HOME SAFETY

For a person with dementia, and the caregiver, home can become a prison. Company may decrease because nobody knows what to say. Doors may be locked from the inside to prevent wandering, and all of the breakables may have to be stored. It may be very difficult to keep up with the household chores. "There's no place like home" often takes on an entirely new meaning!

Caregivers may feel bad about limiting access to particular things or places in the house and yet are torn knowing that records and bills must not get thrown away or hidden in a dresser drawer. Values also influence home safety; one caregiver may value safety more than the person's independence while another knows there is a risk of falling but values a person's ability to move freely in the home.

Regardless, trying to keep your home as safe as possible will become a priority. Try to focus on three things: keep it lit, keep it clear, and keep things in reach. First, make sure all rooms and hallways are well-lit. Add extra lamps or nightlights in darker rooms, and switch to brighter bulbs to make sure your loved one can see things clearly. Try to eliminate clutter, especially on stairs and in walkways. Also make sure the furniture is arranged in such a way that there are easy pathways between rooms. Finally, keep things within easy reach. In the bedroom make sure a lamp and telephone are close to the bed. In the kitchen, keep everyday dishes within reach. No one should be using a stool just to get a drinking glass. Keeping everything in reach without a stool is even better.

5

Dementia changes:

A person may become so forgetful that even a familiar environment becomes confusing. Turning around in a room may be a great enough change to cause disorientation. Other dementia changes include:

- Loss of judgment; people may misinterpret cleaning agents for drinkable liquids.

- Loss of recognition of dangerous situations or activities.

- Inability to call for emergency help, exit a building, or move away from danger.

- Loss of "moving vision," (being able to make sense of things as they move by the person or vice versa).

- Inability to figure out or follow directions even in familiar places.

What to try:

- Dementia-proof your house. Secure cabinets that hold all poisonous liquids and put away tools that may be misused and result in a harmful situation.

- Provide chairs with high enough seat bottoms and arms for support so that the person can easily get up and down.

- Use contrast to draw attention to a favorite chair with a brightly colored throw blanket.

- Put on a new toilet seat or bathroom rug in a contrasting color if your loved one has difficultly locating it.

- Contrast can be used at mealtime too – try a placemat or tablecloth that contrasts with your plates to highlight the food.

- Keep living areas well-lit to help reduce falls.

- Keep windows and blinds open during the day to maximize light.

- Put childproof tops on medication bottles and store out of reach.

- Disarm the stove so the person can't turn it on. (Electric stoves usually have a circuit breaker; gas stoves have removable control knobs).

- Put away all electrical equipment or tools that shouldn't be used without supervision.

- Have grab bars installed near toilet and tub since these are common areas for falls.

- Put away any small rugs that can be trip hazards.

- Use a secure gate at the top and bottom of the steps.

- Don't leave a person with impaired judgment unattended at home or in a car.

- Put labels (words or pictures) on kitchen cabinets or other storage furniture they use frequently.

- Make sure your outdoor walkways are clean and level. Check that any deck or stair railings are sturdy.

5

GIVING UP THE KEYS

In the earlier stages you may have to face the "when-is-it-time-to-stop-driving?" issue. Some people with Alzheimer's disease have good insight about what is happening to them and give up the keys when they feel unsafe or unsure. Others may not have any insight and insist that they can and should continue driving. You may be faced with the task of deciding when driving skills, judgment, and/or visual spatial perceptions have deteriorated. You will have to decide when driving puts the person with dementia and/or others at risk. Driving must be stopped at that time.

Just like many other occasions in caregiving, it is hard to tell someone who may have been driving for 50 or 60 years that they can no longer drive. Driving and independence are closely related in our culture. It is even tougher, but necessary, to take responsibility for not letting a person drive who shouldn't be driving. If you notice your loved one forgetting how to locate familiar places, failing to observe traffic signs, driving at inappropriate speeds, or generally making slow or poor decisions when driving, it may be time to consider if they should still be driving. You don't have to do this alone, but you may be the person who takes the blame. You can expect that the person with dementia will be upset about stopping driving and may focus anger on you. It is a tough spot for both of you. But ultimately, you have to put safety first – for both your loved one and other drivers on the road.

5

Dementia Changes:

- Some individuals in the early stages may still be able to drive safely. However, as dementia progresses, symptoms such as memory loss, visual-spatial disorientation, and cognitive function will decrease over time, all contributing to unsafe driving.

- Slowed reaction times and decision-making abilities will affect driving. The individual may drive too slowly, fail to observe traffic signs, or make errors at intersections.

- As dementia progresses, the individual will lack sound judgement for driving. They may have more accidents or "near-misses" while they are driving.

- Physical changes can make driving more difficult. They may have difficulty seeing pedestrians, signs or other vehicles. They may have more trouble controlling the vehicle, including drifting into other lanes, or parking inappropriately.

- Memory loss can cause individuals to forget their destination, or how to locate familiar places.

What to try:

- Insist that the doctor tell the person and write an order when he or she can no longer drive. This way, you as the caregiver are only following the doctor's orders.

- If you're still met with resistance, perhaps a trusted friend or family member can also express their concerns about your loved ones safety.

- Look into community ride alternatives, or even Uber or Lyft, so that the person who has to give up driving can stay involved in activities away from home.

- If friends are looking for a way to help out, ask them to drive the person to a regular outing, or even just to the grocery store.

- Consult your Division of Motor Vehicles to schedule a driving test which assesses a person's vision, response time, and overall safety behind the wheel. Before testing, consider if your loved one would still continue driving if a license was revoked. This could compound problems if an incident occurs driving without a license.

- Prepare yourself to act decisively when the time comes; watch for signs of impaired judgment, lack of coordination or getting lost in other activities, not just with driving.

- If you won't ride with the person or wouldn't want your children or grandchildren to ride with the person, it is time to stop driving.

- Keep your own set of car keys in a very safe place.

- Sell the other car or disable it. Have a mechanic show you how to remove the distributor cap so the car can't be started without your knowing it. Some people like to sit in it and that is fine as long as it cannot be started or will not move.

- If you're not ready to get rid of the car, ask a friend or neighbor if you can park it at their house. Sometimes what's out of sight is out of mind!

- When the person is riding in the car, always wear seat belts, and use child safety locks if needed.

5

MEDICATION GUIDE

Currently approved medications for Alzheimer's help to alleviate symptoms but do not slow or stop the disease progression. Aricept (donepezil), Razadyne (galantamine) and Exelon (rivastigmine) belong to a class of medications called Cholinesterase Inhibitors and are FDA approved for cognitive enhancement in all stages of Alzheimer's disease. Namenda (memantine) is an NMDA Receptor Antagonist and is FDA approved for treatment of moderate to severe Alzheimer's. Currently, there are no FDA approved medications for treatment of mild cognitive impairment.

Behavioral symptoms, including sleeplessness, wandering, depression, and agitation, are common in dementia and are a major source of burden. Experts agree that medicines to treat behavioral problems should be used only after other strategies have been tried. There are no FDA approved medications for agitation or aggression in dementia. An important rule of thumb when prescribing behavioral medications is "start low and go slow." Every patient is unique and responses to behavioral interventions and medications can vary widely.

- Visit the National Institute on Aging, Alzheimer's Disease Education and Referral (ADEAR) center for more information on current treatment approaches focused on helping people maintain mental function and manage behavioral symptoms of Alzheimer's disease.

5

Research towards the discovery of disease modifying or preventative treatments is advancing and holds great promise for the future. This important research is dependent on the people who voluntarily agree to participate in clinical trials and studies. To learn more about AD treatment and research, consider joining a prevention registry.

- Alzheimer Prevention Trial (APT) Webstudy - aptwebstudy.org

- Alzheimer's Prevention Registry- endalznow.org

- Healthy Brains- healthybrains.org

- Brain Health Registry- brainhealthregistry.org

Dementia Changes:

- Alzhemer's disease is a gradually progressive disorder. The most common reasons for sudden or rapid decline in AD are infection, adverse reaction to medications, or environmental changes.

- Even people with mild memory loss symptoms require assistance and supervision with medication administration.

- In general, only one medication change should be made at a time. This allows for better assessment of benefit or adverse reaction to a dosage change or a new medication.

- Always review all of the medications that your loved one is taking (including over-the-counter medications and supplements) with your doctor at each appointment.

- Do not assume that over-the-counter medications and supplements are universally safe. Non-prescription medications or supplements can be harmful and may have dangerous interactions with other medications.

Things to do:

- Use a weekly pill box and pre-pour medications weekly. Offer daily reminders for taking medications. This allows for closer supervision and helps to minimize errors while maintaining the person's involvement in their care.

- Keep an accurate list of medications including dosages and start dates. Bring the medication list to all medical appointments.

  - List all allergies to medications. Write them down when you learn about them, include the name of the medication and the type of reaction the person had to it. Knowing that the person is allergic to "some antibiotic" is not enough.

  - If the person has tried various drugs for a particular problem, tell the doctor what they were and what the effects were.

  - If the doctor prescribes a medicine, ask the following questions:

  - What is the medication for?

  - When should it be given? (Some meds are ineffective on an empty stomach; others have to be given between meals.)

  - Are there side effects? If so, what is normal and what should be reported to the physician?

  - Can the medicine be crushed or capsules opened if administering a pill is difficult? Does it come in a liquid form that might be easier to give?

  - If you miss a dose - do you take it the next time, or skip it?

  - How long will the person be on the medication before it becomes effective?

- Use caution when considering purchasing supplements for boosting or preserving memory that you've seen or heard advertised on TV, the radio, or the internet. Often there is little or

5

no basis for claims that are made and someone may be profiting financially at your expense. Always check the source and consult with your physician prior to taking any new medications or supplements.

- Alcohol is a drug. People become more sensitive to alcohol as they age and alcohol can contribute to memory loss and falls. In general, alcohol use should be limited to 1 to 2 drinks per day (e.g., 1 to 2 ounces of liquor, 1 to 2 six ounce glasses of wine, 1 to 2 twelve ounce beers). You should discuss alcohol use with your physician and follow their recommendation regarding alcohol use or abstinence.

- Every medication has two names, a generic and a trade or brand name. For example, Aricept is the trade name for donepezil, while donepezil is the generic name for Aricept. The active ingredient in the generic and brand medication is the same. The generic version of a medication is generally less expensive and becomes available after the drug has been on the market for a period of time. Consult with you doctor to determine whether generic or brand medication is best for your loved one. Be careful not to administer the same medication twice.

About Insight Memory Care Center

Insight Memory Care Center, formerly Alzheimer's Family Day Center, is a nonprofit adult day health and resource center providing specialized care, support, and education for individuals with Alzheimer's disease and other memory impairments, their families, caregivers, and the community. Serving Northern Virginia since 1984, Insight offers a spectrum of holistic care, with a vision of a community where those affected by memory impairments can achieve the highest quality of life.

Insight's adult day health center provides a safe, engaging, and therapeutic environment for individuals with mid to later stage memory impairment. It is the only dementia-specific day center in the DC metro area and still the only adult day health center in Northern Virginia with programs for people in the later stages of dementia. For those in the early stages, Insight offers social engagement programs to maximize capabilities, and provide support for loved ones to adjust to changing family dynamics. Additionally, our innovative education and support programs provide caregiver classes, community trainings, professional seminars, support groups, and individual consultations. These programs help family members remain confident and effective in their caregiving roles and increase awareness and understanding of the disease in the community.

We hope this guide can share at least a small piece of what we do. For additional resources, please visit InsightMCC.org or call us at 703-204-4664.

CPSIA information can be obtained
at www.ICGtesting.com
Printed in the USA
LVHW071034170622
721536LV00018B/406